*poems of life and death by*
# Gary Lucero

I miss you, Mom.
Thank you for always supporting me.

Thanks to Lisa McCoy, not only for her amazing editing skills, but also, for helping me to understand the art of writing and for encouraging me to believe in myself.

Thanks to Kate at Westley Enterprises for her marvelous book design.

Thank you, Janis.
For listening.

Inspired by the greatest singer/songwriters of all time:

Neil Young.
Jon Anderson.
Pete Townsend.
Roger Waters.

This is a work of fiction. Names, characters, places, and incidents are the product of the author's imagination or are used fictitiously. Any resemblance to actual persons, living or dead, events, or locales is entirely coincidental.

Copyright © 2024 Gary A. Lucero

All rights reserved. No part of this book may be reproduced or used in any manner without written permission of the copyright owner except for the use of quotations in a book review.

# Contents

## The Abyss of Time — 1

Lightness Round ................................................... 3
So, I Turn Away .................................................. 5
Subsistence ......................................................... 7
A Fallen Victim to the Lost .................................. 9
Writers of Storm ................................................. 11
When I Flew ...................................................... 13
Stones ................................................................ 15
Simple ................................................................ 17
In Letting Go ..................................................... 19

## Realm of the Dead — 21

Life Then Ends .................................................. 23
She Claims ......................................................... 25
Son of Sadness ................................................... 27
To No Longer .................................................... 31
No Hope ............................................................ 33
End It Stays ....................................................... 35
In the Twilight ................................................... 37
Life Is Short ....................................................... 39
Come What May ............................................... 41

## And So It Is With Heroes — 43

The Realm ......................................................... 45
Mount Polaris .................................................... 47
The Mighty ........................................................ 49

The King .................................................................. 51

The Dead One ......................................................... 53

The Hero ................................................................. 57

The Lost One .......................................................... 59

The Peasant ............................................................. 61

The See-er of the Stones ........................................ 63

The Vile Witch ....................................................... 65

The Arms Merchant ............................................... 69

The Demon Knight ................................................ 73

And So It Is With Heroes ...................................... 75

# Thank You            79

# Contact Information    81

# About The Author      83

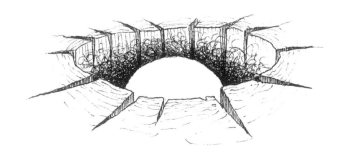

# The Abyss of Time

## Lightness Round

The lightness of youth
The intensity of yearning
The transient expectation
The beginning of beginning

And, with it, angst
Forward march
Backward progress
Never relenting
Always searching

And although the want moves onward
The light can't catch
The narrow ridge of time
It spills and tails round

Darkness enters
Rearing its unwanted head
Forever searching
To bind and to foil
To find and forget

Time slows
The light gathers into gloom
The mind fogs and bedraggles
The yearning slows to a crawl

And though it doesn't stop
It hesitates
And in that moment
The light escapes
Never to appear again

And youth is gone
Forever abandoned
And in the darkness, one stumbles
Falls into the abyss of time
And there is no escape

# So, I Turn Away

As I stare into the mirror
I wonder what I've become
What sickness has seeped within
What foul menace has gripped my soul

What might it do to me?
Consume my entire being?
Or will true hatred erupt?
And a terror be unleashed?

I could be a killer who stalks his prey
Hiding in the shadows
Waiting for his next victim
So that he may feast upon their soul

I must turn away
Conserve what small bit of humanity I have
Before it's consumed by the evil
And the ugly truth escapes

It's better to ignore the potential
It's never good to tempt the unknown
Life should be lived in ignorance
One must never know what darkness lies within

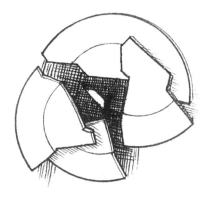

## Subsistence

A subsistence of half-truths and petty lies
Of unfulfilled emotions
Of failed expectations
And of never-ending disappointment

A subsistence of underwhelming performance
Of missed opportunities
Of oppressive depression
And of half-assed attempts at living life

A subsistence of squandered resources
Of poor bargains
Of wasted breath
And of a failure to comprehend what's required

A subsistence of mind-numbing stupidity
Of wrong conclusions
Of missed conversational cues
And of a total lack of wisdom

And most of all, a subsistence of doubt
Of never believing wholeheartedly
Of never trusting the truth
And of never taking a chance on life

## A Fallen Victim to the Lost

You lie down in your bed at night
Your eyes close
You enter the realm of dream
And watch as it unfolds

You walk alone, the brightness shimmering
You stumble forward, unsure of your next steps
Then your vision darkens, fading light and memories
And then blackness, and you see the veil draw near

The images come, as your breath fades
And in the darkness, the light slowly returns
And as you walk, she is standing there
A ghostly image, translucent in serenity

She's a farmer's widow
A lost and twisted soul
She stands still and quiet, never fading
Her eyes pierce yours, and you cannot look away

You shudder, the vision flickers in the shadows
Then she turns, and heads for the burning fields
You wonder, pondering what and where you are
The light then gathers, and the mist descends again

There are moving passages, and calls to other days
Wanton memories, of missing scenes and times
You venture forth, but you never see the same again
You wake from dreams, of time and space surreal

Blinking, you think of her and strain
Was she real, and who could she have been?
Was she a fallen victim to the lost?
Of future's past and present, of time stood still?

There's no knowing what the dreams could see
There are far too many patterns in play
So, you turn about and shut your eyes again
Time to see what next the night might bring

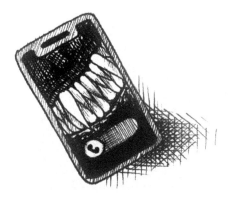

## Writers of Storm

Magical adventures
Great holidays
Lost in the forest
In unmarked graves

Whitewashed but soiled
Reptilian clones
Invading our countries
Our lives and our homes

Wandering pragmatists
Censored though proud
Spouting collusions
But never out loud

Man on the street
Drones in the sky
Raining down terrors
That seduce and divide

And mangled monsters
Whose teeth glitter white
Listen in on phone calls
In the dawn an' twilight

Malevolent masters?
Or scum sucking whores?
They preach from the pulpit
They walk on all fours

They lie and they cheat
They collect money for fun
They insist on our freedom
While pointing a gun

They sell us our souls
They guide us to doom
They give us no answers
They build us a tomb

They ride in black limos
They sit in white houses
They carry the plague
Like little shy mouses

And yet they do glitter
They look bright and so warm
They're nothing if not
The writers of storm

# When I Flew

When I flew through the clouds
Burning lights taped to my armpits
Mice skittered to and fro
And yet you sat stammering

When I flew through the archway
Jesus hanging from my feet
You laughed, callous in contempt
But he was not amused

When I flew through the air
Sights set on star systems unseen
You misjudged the navigational inputs
And I crashed and burned

When I flew inside the Earth's core
My eyes watering from the elements
And I found the item you had lost
You never thanked me for its return

And so, I flew through the escape hatch
My mind's eye otherwise preoccupied
And as water passed below me
You couldn't care less

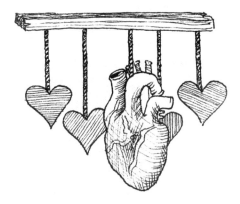

## Stones

Let stones fly about this place
Hearts on strings that end in miles of sadness
If we are to return
Then let the band begin to sound its tune
We shall dance
And the fall's coldness will whisk us away
The heart will be strong again
And the skies will end their gloom

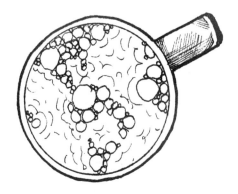

# Simple

The history of our universe
The glory of the page
A million, mindless, boggling idiots
All in a rage

A fearless, fruitful, farmer
Veteran of the war
A man with true intentions
Sitting in a bar

Wondering fringe of absurdity
Lonely, desperate folk
Complete entertainment
Just dying for a joke

Fathers, mothers, kids
They wander aimlessly
Divorce, rape, and incest
Their only plea

A nation where villains lurk
At every bend
They call us daily
Asking to be our friend

Yet weeping fills our hearts
Lies rip apart our lives
And in the end
The simple are the only who'll survive

## In Letting Go

In feeling emotion

In sensing the patterns of stars and the signaling of twilight

In letting go

In falling faster through a spiraling staircase of dreams

And in finding, finally, something to hold onto

One finds him or herself

# Realm of the Dead

# Life Then Ends

As we circle the drain of our existence
And approach the realm of the dead
As we navigate the roads of life
We see the signs of our end

We try to cast our gaze above us
Beyond the dimness of our domain
Straining to find some hope
Some measure of forgiveness

But our eyes are old and worthless
Unable to focus on anything that lingers
Unable to find hope where none exists
And unwilling to stir the heart

So, we fall deeper into sorrow
Deeper into the realm of the dead
Deeper into the nights of eternity
And slip into oblivion

With nothing left and no one to help us
With all eyes turned toward the darkness
With all hearts hardened and broken
Life then ends

## She Claims

As she opens to accept the offering
As she tugs at his skin
As she swallows him
As she makes him her own

Not a willing subject
But a captive one

As she forms him anew
A transition from flesh to earth
Death folds in on him
And nourishes her
Life springs from within her
And the continuity of it all proceeds

He's another claimed by her
Another changed by her
Another merged by her
Another formed by her anew

## Son of Sadness

Sad notes streaming
The sorrowed tune
Minded briefly
Ended soon

Cat-like wonders
Breath, life, earth
She stared eerily
As she gave it birth

And it fell
Eyes opened wide
Reading infinities
All so wise

Stars aligned
Words constrained
Thoughts are pounding
In a mind enflamed

Aimed at tangent
Without a smile
A rambling regent
That walks for miles

A case of plenty
Of careless breeze
Of stifled stillness
And ill disease

And it ventured
It rose upon
With golden tassels
With muted song

And it conquered
And it turned
Villages visited
Were crimson burned

Fires aplenty
Death so still
Fires consuming
As mountains reel

But if Sodom sought him
If Hell did reach
If death betrayed him
If defeat did breach

From Satan's blossom
From begin to end
From son of sadness
To death's best friend

From crown of victory
To end of days
From razer of armies
To eyes of haze

From mighty conqueror
From the son that fell
To the withered remains
In the golden pale

# To No Longer

To cast myself aloft

To fly and plummet

To glide towards Mother Earth

To feel the wind whip and tug and tear

To see the ground as it rises to meet me

To know the end is near

To crash

To lie in a heap, alone and dead

To sever myself from humanity

To no longer fear

To no longer love

To no longer hate

To no longer

# No Hope

In the champagne of death
I find my body strewn
Lying in a bath of piss and shit and blood
With open wounds and a fallen soul

But I continue my journey
Oblivious to my current state
Never conscious of my own death
Unwilling to admit defeat

Then I reach the end of the lonely road
With shadowy figures awaiting my arrival
Solemn glances receive me
And realization dawns

This is the end
No more chances at redemption
Only oblivion and perdition
Damnation for an eternity

And with no hope
I no longer have choice
I resign myself
It's time to depart

I await my name to be called
And walk through the gate
No friendly faces greet me
Only the eternal fires

It's not like I didn't know
I'd spent my life in waste
Gave all to the devil
And none to those who cared

And now this grim fate
It's immovable
It consumes me
It has reclaimed my sorry soul

And thus, I died
But there is no rest
No peace, nor love
No good end

As is fitting
Why waste heaven on a good for nothing?
I don't deserve better
I deserve nothing at all

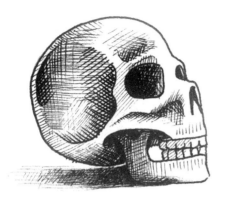

# End It Stays

Life given
End it stays
We're left unwanted
Tired, exhausted
We surrender

Minds alone
Tamed through temptation
Standing without reason
Cold, unwoven
And unable to fathom

So, wishes for death
An end to justify the means
God strike us
Kill, deal
When nothing else can

We attempt to scream
Yet we're speechless
Teeth shattered
Fragments, breaking
Tongues cut out

There's no escape
No tunnel to end
Just carrion crawlers
In our grave, our prison
Feasting upon our worthless remains

We're surrounded by sorrow
The air stands still
The putrefaction begins
The gloom, it gathers
And takes us into nothing

And in nothing
We are reclaimed
Our souls received
And death binds us all
Rewards us, brings peace
And in peace we find the end

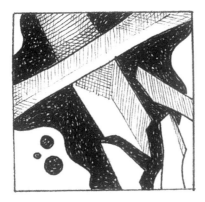

# In the Twilight

In the twilight effervescence knell
We stood, brave and loyal
And in standing, we knew, soldiers we
Ready to fight and die for our King

In the raging, mangled heap of fire
Dragons' flames licking at our blades
We never doubted nor faltered
We died often, and we died well

In the graves, shallow as they were
Maggots consuming our flesh
We lay, alone and without our maker's breath
We were but a memory of a battle now forgotten

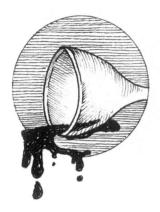

# Life Is Short

Life's transient
Fleeting at best
A wink of the eye

Yet we must continue
Forever on we struggle

Thus, we live

Never knowing
Never realizing
But always sure that life is short

# Come What May

While some hold on to barely an existence
It's unfathomable to me
To live as if in death
To wake to darkness
To wander alive through the graves

So many refuse
To find peace and solemnity
To end their struggles
To face what waits beyond

I'd rather go
Transition to nothingness
Become ash
Because once life holds no more pleasures
There's no reason for existence

I'll not be a walking dead man
Let death come when it may

*And So It Is With Heroes*

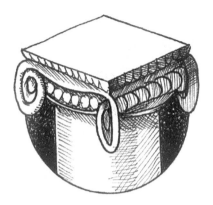

# The Realm

The Realm has stood for ages
It is as old as the gods
It has stood through sieges
Through freezes and thaws

And when evil pounced upon it
And when death knocked its door
The Realm stood firm
Its foundation solid and sure

And kings have blessed it
And kings have let it wane
And kings have made it prosper
And blessed it once again

But it is not the one who dwells within it
Nor the one who bares the sword
It is not the one who claims it
With their deeds or their word

Because no matter if in glory
And no matter if in shame
The Realm remains as pure
As the day it became

The Realm brings the sunshine
The Realm brings the dawn
The Realm lights the world
And the world spins on and on

And though man falls and rises
The Realm has steady state
The Realm stands with virtue
The Realm stands with fate

# Mount Polaris

On her summit sits the See-er of the Stones
Whisps of clouds and cold 'round her head
At her feet lies naught but broken bones
In her depths is naught but dread

Giants and dragons help keep her guard
Goblins and ogres mine her for gold
Witches and warlocks give their regard
None grow weary nor do they grow old

Champions climb her storied heights
But most fall before they reach her peak
Only the bravest maintain their light
Only the strongest do dare seek

With swords raised do heroes stand tall
Armed to defend and to attack
To the hardiest of them do monsters fall
Or do drive them back

But Mount Polaris dies hard indeed
It is said she is unable to fail
At most, heroes make her bleed
But more oft they turn tail

Thus, she stands, tall and proud
Though quiet, without pretense
Not that she need be very loud
To keep up her strong defense

# The Mighty

Perched in the clouds above The Realm
The Mighty stand court
Gods with infinite power
Toying with man for sport

They hear the prayers of the people
And the supplications of the poor
The pleading of peons
Which They choose to ignore

But to The King They do listen
They hear his prayers for aid
They help smite his many foes
And bless his holy blade

Meanwhile, plagues kill his people
And starvation ends their lives
Their farms swarmed by goblins
And their throats cut by knives

But only The King has Their blessing
He has the ear of the gods
And for that he gives much thanks
For what is and what was

For the rain and the snow
For the grain and the cows
For health and good fortune
For the here and the now

For soldiers and workers
For lovers and friends
For gold and for silver
And a reign he hopes will not end

# The King

They called my father, The Ruthless
And they call me the same
But the people all love me
They chant and praise my dear name

I have waged battle against tyrants
And battles against fools
I have conquered evil dominions
And crushed those too weak to rule

My throne is encrusted with silver
With gold, diamonds, and jade
The halls are hallowed and holy
And protected by blade

My knights all surround me
As do pike men, archers, and spies
Swordsmen at the ready
Wanting and willing to die

And though I have fathered many
With wives, maidens, and whores
When I am dead only one shall succeed me
Only one shall be Lord

As of present he is but a babe
But in time he will grow
And one day The Ruthless will he be
And peace and justice he will sow

My son will be mighty
He will be just and he will be fair
He will crush all his enemies
All those that shall dare

His army will be powerful
Absolute will be his rule
The people will love him
They will call him their jewel

And though my death will bring sadness
It will not be the end
The Realm will live on forever
Never shall it rend

# The Dead One

Under Mount Polaris
In a fiery pit of gloom
Out of the darkness comes
A dim but deadly plume

From the miasma The Dead One rises
As a champion of hate
All evil gathers 'round it
To tempt The Mighty at fate

It is a being not unlike a god
Its home is hell
It whispers terrible secrets
As the evil within it swells

How was it created?
How did it arise?
Hatred was its mother
It has her cold dead eyes

And from it others spawned
The Vile Witch arose
As did The Lost One
The force of evil grows

It roams the countryside
In and out of hamlets does it rise
Possessing peasants and merchants
Forcing their hearts to despise

And though The King protests it
Girds his armies to defend The Realm
And although heroes fight it
They are overwhelmed

But is The Dead One unstoppable?
Is fate a sealed tome?
Surely all cannot be lost
And we are not all alone

So, continue to fight the good fight
To quell evil where it stirs
Slay the evil dragons!
Flail thy sword in bloody blurs!

The Dead One may epitomize evil
But surely it can be killed
The ungodly stirrings silenced
And all its minions stilled

May The Mighty guide us!
May the gods give us power
May The King lead us!
In this most desperate of hours

Raise thy swords all heroes!
Be the promise of The Realm
Let not evil take us!
Do not let it overwhelm!

# The Hero

With The Mighty as my witness
I have sworn to protect my King
To lay down my life in his stead
To kneel before him, to kiss his ring

With every ounce of my courage
I shall always smite his foes
I shall protect the kingdom
And evil shall I expose

And though The Dead One may beseech me
I shall never give it quarter
I pray The Mighty protect me
To help me protect our borders

May The King live forever
May The Realm endure as well
May The Dead One be forever vanquished
In the ubiquity of hell

May The Mighty always bless us
In life as well as in death
And may I always serve our King
Until my last and dying breath

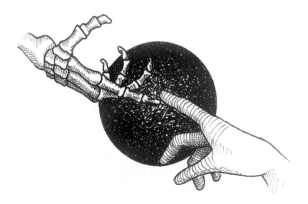

# The Lost One

Once a friend of wisdom
And a subject of The King
He ventured into Mount Polaris
And evil within him did spring

He lost his name and memories
He lost his spirit and soul
He lost his will to live life
He lost his will to know

He lost all his family
He lost all his friends
He lost his community
And came to his own end

He glommed onto The Dead One
He gave it his hand
He saw the rotting evil
And still he joined its band

He saw The Dead One's creations
He heard all its lies
He knew its intentions for mankind
He sensed his own demise

But that made him more determined
To lose himself in whole
To give himself to evil
And to further all its goals

And so, he lost himself completely
He disappeared in truth
In both mind and form he is missing
So completely did he loose

And so, he came to an end
And he came to not be
And now when we look upon him
No more can we see he

# The Peasant

Life was supposed to improve
The King said we'd get chickens to boil
But we got nothing in our pots
And nothing grows from our soil

What are we to do?
We've got no way to fight
The guard would kill us in an instant
We've got no hope and no rights

We be the common folk
The scum of the earth
No one cares much about us
We're naught of any worth

While The King sits so proud
On his royal throne
Flanked by guards and beauties
We're left alone

We got nothing fancy
And nothing much to eat
No one to protect us
We have to be light on our feet

We're tilling the soil
Or begging on the streets
Dying of common pestilence
Or the odd, random decease

Sometimes we be cannon fodder
Soldiers on the front line
And sometimes we be forgotten
On no one's bleedin' mind

And although he makes us promises
The King can't deliver
The Mighty never regard us
We've no caregiver

We might as well pray to The Dead One
That it send The Demon Knight
Hope for him to kill us all
And end our endless plight

'Cause help is not coming
Not tomorrow nor today
Starvation's all we've got
And it's here to stay

## The See-er of the Stones

You cannot see the See-er of the Stones
But it can see you
Even when you are all alone
You are in its full view

It is the eyes of The Dead One
Seeing from within its gloom
It can see when there is a setting sun
As if it were high noon

No use in hiding from its eyes
As it has none
It does not need them to spy
Nor from it can you run

The See-er of the Stones is everywhere
Inside and out
And though it cannot hear you there
It can see you without doubt

And upon The Mighty you may calleth
Or you might implore The King
Whisper curses under your breath
Yet it sees everything

You are never safe from its sight
There is no escape from its dread
Even when you think it knows not your thoughts
It sees inside your head

# The Vile Witch

She was known as Lolli Gallagher
And she was sweet as she could be
Her life one of peace and love
Helping those who were in need

She was once known as a wisdom
She dabbled with the herbs
Helping folk who felt poorly
Or were suffering from nerves

Then one day she wandered into the woods
But never did she come back
She fell into a pit of gloom
Filled with evil pitch as black

There The Dead One swayed her
Taught her all that it knew
Gave her power o'er life and death
And recipes to brew

"First put poison mushrooms in the pot
Then spider's eggs and hemlock root
Next a human kidney and liver
Lastly, the eye of newt

Stir it all to concoct the potion
As vile as it is strong
One sip will break a man in two
Even the strongest cannot last long"

With her spells, incantations, and potions
For The Dead One she does bid
Swaying the minds of men and women
For evil they should live

She is now corrupt
Her mind filled with wicked plans
She cackles at the thought of capturing folk
And sawing off their hands

The Vile Witch has lost her life
She is evil and without heart
She is filled only with hate
Only sorrow does she impart

The Dead One commands her every move
It controls her every thought
It has erased all the good in her
And turned her life to naught

And so, she does its bidding
Works towards the end of man
No more is she a wisdom
That is not The Dead One's plan

# The Arms Merchant

I have never held a sword in my hand
Nor have I worn chain upon my chest
I have never seen a monster's glare
Nor by ghosts have I been molest

I am in my shop from dawn to dusk
I buy arms that I sell and trade
I drive the hardest of bargains
I never spend; I always save

The King's armies buy my weapons
The King's coin fills my coffers
The King's soldiers bear my arms
The King's buyers accept my offers

They never ask me questions
They trust me implicitly
They doubt not my virtue
Though filled with virtue I not be

I am a merchant of the finest class
I have amassed riches quite untold
My wife knows not of my success
She thinks us poor and growing old

My children wear rags to their lessons
My wife scrimps and she saves
She never asks me for money
She would never be so brave

As my piles of coin grow larger
As my family struggles to exist
As my ego reaches new horizons
As I become the best I insist

As I near my death age
And hold onto every cent
Knowing my family will see none of it
I know my mind is bent

So while monsters do not haunt me
The threat of losing is always near
And while business has never been better
I still live my life in fear

Fear that profits will lessen
Fear that I will spend too much
Fear that I will charge too little
Fear that I will lose my touch

Fear that evil will subside
Fear the armies will stop buying
Fear of my life coming to an end
Fear the King will find out that I am lying

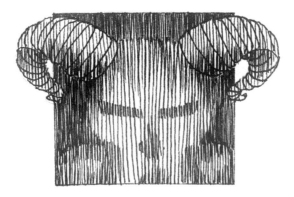

# The Demon Knight

He stands as tall as two men
In armor black as night
His presence brings dread to all
He is The Demon Knight

His sword forged of evil
His plate forged of greed
His mind oh so feeble
And Death his only need

He roams with a yearning
Killing his only desire
He stalks prey relentlessly
His business is dire

Death beckons he come nearer
To succumb its foul embrace
And so, he kills every man he finds
At his own slow but steady pace

He marches as do soldiers
Because once he was
Before The Dead One slayed him
And with death gave him pause

So now he is a monster
Spreading evil, fear, and death
No longer one that is living
No longer takes a single breath

His life has been taken
And life he does take
His mind has been broken
So others does he break

The Demon Knight wanders
The Demon Knight kills
The Demon Knight slaughters
In death and fear he does thrill

## And So It Is With Heroes

We stand on Mount Polaris
With dragon's heads at our feet
We have smote foes far grander than ourselves
And thousands did we lead

Our arrows pummeled witches
Our axes beheaded trolls
Our swords felled mighty giants
The blood spurted and it whorled

And though we conquered evil
We left our loved ones all alone
We ignored and even slighted them
We let our children freely roam

We were careful to find wrongdoers
And careful to take them down
But we failed to account for those who loved us
And we failed to stick around

And now insanity grips them
They are loose or corrupt or torn
Their minds are missing pieces
Their consciences well worn

And we face the truth of folly
And we see we have fallen down
We know that we are guilty
And that our punishment is sound

We shall grow old like the wicked
We shall die and see the end
We shall look into the mirror
And see foes but no good friends

We will endure children who fail us
And wives who hate
We will smile not, nor enjoy life
Death will come far too late

And so it is with heroes
With those who brandish swords
And so it is with cowards
Those who brandish only words
And so it is with tyrants
With rulers, merchants, and men
And so it is with heroes
And so it is in the end

# Thank You

Thank you for reading *In Letting Go*. I hope you enjoyed it. If you have a moment, please review it on your bookstore of choice.

Your reviews help others to find my work and help me to improve my writing.

# Contact Information

You can find me online and contact me through the following:

garylucerowriter.com

contact@garylucerowriter.com

Facebook @garylucerowriter

Instagram @garylucerowriter

# *About The Author*

Gary Lucero is a Latino author born and raised in Albuquerque, New Mexico. A Hispanic father and Basque mother provided a loving family for their four children, of which Gary is the youngest.

His household was brimming with cats and his mother welcomed the neighborhood kids into their home and treated them with the same love and respect she showed to her own children.

Gary loved music from an early age. He appreciated his parent's country-western and Mexican music, was an addict of AM radio as a child, but it was rock music that changed his life.

Musical artists such as Neil Young and Yes swept through Gary's consciousness with vast landscapes of images concerning social change and political conflict that colored his earliest poetry and helped form his philosophies and outlook on life.

To this day, Gary's favorite poets are songwriters.

In grade school, Gary wandered his neighborhood in West Albuquerque with a Canon SLR slung around his neck. It wasn't just photography that intrigued him, though, as he was also enamored with the technology that made cameras work.

In his early twenties, Gary purchased a primitive personal computer, the Commodore VIC-20, and that started his life-long love of computers. To this day, he is a technology enthusiast.

Gary has worked in software development for the past 35 years, has a passionate love of progressive rock music, and has filled his home with dogs. He writes poetry and is currently piecing together a book of his short stories.

Milton Keynes UK
Ingram Content Group UK Ltd.
UKHW022017240924
448733UK00016B/979